A GUIDE
TO
SUCCESSFUL PUBLIC
SPEAKING

Howard Wade

Easyway Guides

Easyway Guides

ISBN 1900694 51 4

Cover design by Hamilton Design

Printed by Polestar Wheaton, Exeter.

A GUIDE TO SUCCESSFUL PUBLIC SPEAKING

CONTENTS

Public Speaking-Roles and Events

INTRODUCTION

Many times we have watched people stand up in front of others and deliver a speech or presentation. Politicians, actors, managers, a whole variety of people whose living depends on presenting to others in public. Often, the person speaking makes it look so effortless, as though speaking in front of others is the most natural thing in the world. For some it is. However, this book is designed for the majority who find public speaking and presenting in front of others a nerve-wracking experience.

There are a number of key aspects that are fundamental to the art of public speaking and making presentations. Without a doubt the two most important are the person presenting and the nature of the material. This book concentrates heavily on these areas, offering invaluable advice.

In addition, advice on the use of visual aids and on the nature of the setting in which the public speaker will deliver his or her address is offered and also instruction on making the presentation and audience management.

Overall, this book will benefit those people who are new to the area of public speaking and making presentations. However, it will also benefit those who are more experienced but need a refresher on the art of presenting.

Effective public speaking is an art and a skill and the rewards to those who can become effective presenters are enormous. It is hoped that this book will go some way to developing the skills and abilities needed.

1

THE ART OF PUBLIC SPEAKING

Public speaking is very much an art and a skill that can be mastered by anyone. It is true to say that some people may be initially better equipped for the role of public speaker than others, by virtue of their own particular personality type. However, the truly effective public speaker learns the craft and applies certain techniques that generally derive from experience.

In this book I will be alluding to the person who has to deliver a speech or present a seminar, rather than the professional teacher. It is the person who is not constantly engaged in addressing groups who will most benefit from what is contained within. All of the points raised in this chapter will be explored in depth later on in this book.

The person and the material

There are two vital ingredients in public speaking. The first is very much the person delivering the speech or other material to a group. The second is the nature of the material being delivered.

The Person

For some people, standing in front of an audience, whatever the size, is not a real problem. For others however, the very thought of exposing oneself to a group of people, and being so vulnerable, is a nightmare best avoided.

When trying to put this into context it is important to remember that, when we communicate as part of a group, or simply on a one to-one basis with another, then we interact primarily through speech and body language. We are often confident within ourselves because we feel secure in that we are part of a group interacting and that all eyes are not on us alone, at least not for a protracted period.

The situation is very different indeed when we are alone and faced with a group of people, strangers or not, and we have to present material. It means that we have to assume responsibility and take the lead and communicate successfully to others. Nervousness is very often the result when placed in this situation, because, until we can make contact with the audience and establish a rapport, we are very much alone and feel vulnerable.

Obviously, there are a number of factors influencing the levels of confidence and differences in attitude between people, such as the nature and type of the person and their background, their past experience, both within the family and in the world of work and numerous other experiences besides. All these will affect a persons ability to become an effective public speaker.

This publication cannot completely erase your nervousness. It cannot change your personality overnight. However, what it can certainly do is to raise your awareness to the root of that feeling in the context of public speaking and to help you become more confident.

It can also show you that, whatever your personality type, you can become a successful public speaker by applying certain fundamental techniques.

Why do we feel nervous?

There are a number of reasons why we may feel nervous. You need to question yourself and ask yourself why. Was the sight of so many faces in front of you enough to frighten you and make you lose your self-confidence or are you plagued by the memory of previous mistakes? You need to remember that you change and develop as a person as you gain more experience and that past mistakes do not mean that you will repeat them.

Let's face it, most of us will experience nerves in a situation which is stressful to us. This is totally normal and quite often we become anxious and charged with adrenaline that drives us on. When it comes to speaking in public the adrenaline can be positive but excessive nerves are negative and can lead to aggression.

Fundamentally, the key to successful public speaking is the acquisition of confidence coupled with assertiveness that leads to the ability to effectively control a situation. If you are assertive and you know your subject matter you are likely to be confident and in control and less likely to feel nervous.

Be prepared!

Directly related to the above, preparation is everything and to feel confident with your material means that you are half way there already. Although I will be expanding on preparation a little later, there are a few fundamental tips that can help you along.

You should listen to speakers, particularly good speakers as often as possible in order to gain tips. Notice the way that good and effective speakers construct their sentences. Listen for the eloquence. Remember, shorter sentences have a lot more impact and are easier to grasp than long sentences. They also act as a discipline for the speaker in that they will prevent him or her from straying off the point.

Another very important factor when approaching the day of your presentation is preparing yourself psychologically. Convince yourself that you are looking forward to the speech and that you will do well no matter what. Convey this to your audience as you open your presentation, say that you are glad to be with them and that you hope that this goes well for all. This reinforces a feeling of goodwill and will express itself through your body language and your voice.

Finally, one of the main aids to effective public speaking is *experience* and that only comes through practice so it is essential that you take every opportunity offered you to sharpen your skills in this area.

In the next two chapters I will be concentrating on presentation and style. Fundamental to preparation as a speaker is the ability to relax and focus your mind and body on the task ahead.

Before you turn to chapter two, however, you should read the key points from chapter one overleaf.

KEY POINTS FROM CHAPTER ONE

- The truly effective public speaker learns the craft and applies certain techniques which generally derive from experience

- There are two vital ingredients in public speaking. The first is the person and the second is the material

- The key to successful public speaking is the acquisition of knowledge coupled with assertiveness which leads to the ability to control and direct a situation

- Listen to effective and successful speakers in order to gain tips

- Prepare yourself psychologically for your speech. Put yourself in a positive frame of mind!

2
KNOWING YOUR AUDIENCE

The one golden rule when it comes to speaking in public is that you should always keep your audience in mind. Whatever the reason, and whatever the objectives of the speaker, every speech must meet the expectations of the audience. The speech must be tailored to suit their needs, interests and levels. If you address the audience's needs and use language that they will understand, then you will go a long way towards a successful speech.

Useful questions to ask whoever has invited you to speak are:

- Will the audience be made up of mostly men or will it be cross gender?

- What age group is the audience?

- What is their interest in the proceedings?

- What do they do for a living, how economically successful are they?

- What racial and cultural background do they come from?

- Are they attending on a voluntary or involuntary basis?

You may also be able to contact a speaker who has addressed the same audience and ask them what they believe to be the main points from their experience.

When you are studying the information gathered in these ways, try to put yourself in the audience's shoes. Try to identify the motivations and aspirations of your group, which can be broken down, broadly, into three areas: their interest; their level of experience; their needs.

Audience interest

Every audience that attends an event does so because they have an interest in the proceedings. If you as a speaker can engage that interest, then you will have gone a long way in grabbing and keeping the audience's attention when you speak.

The audience at a conference may be the members of the same profession, and so they have a common interest in staying up to date with issues that relate to their business. Write down why you think your audience is interested in attending the event at which you will be speaking. Then decide how your subject and your objectives can be reconciled with what you believe your audience's interests to be.

Level of expertise

Each audience can be profiled in terms of its educational background and expertise. Some audiences are drawn from a particular profession. Therefore, if speaking about that profession, they will be considered to be experts.

However, if the same people constitute an audience and you are speaking about a subject unrelated to their profession then they will not be expert. Most audiences, however, are mixed in terms of their expertise. Write down what you consider your audience's level of expertise in the subject at hand is likely to be, and then decide how this will affect your speech.

Meeting the needs of the audience

Every audience has its 'expertise' profile and its own interest in attending the event. Join an audience in its common interest and speak to it in terms that it can understand, and you are well on your way towards achieving your objectives. However, the real key to winning an audience's attention and making them ready to listen, is to understand their needs and incorporate them into your speech.

Psychologists believe that modern-day people have a number of needs, and that these are basically the same for everyone:

- Economic-the need to be financially better off or secure.

- Physical comfort-the need to be warm and fed, but also be unconfined, to be free to roam.

- Psychological-the need to be free from worry and psychological anxiety.

- Acceptance-the need to feel that other people accept them as part of a social group.

- Exploration-the need to know and understand new facts and concepts.

- Political security-the need to be free from political constraint.

Each member of an audience comes to an event with all of these needs. They expect the speaker to fulfil one or more or to tell them something that will help them to do so. Identifying the audience's particular needs and speaking with them in mind will gain their attention and keep their interest. It is vital that you fulfil the audience's expectations if your speech is to be a success.

If you perceive a group to have mixed needs, then you should try to speak to as many of those needs as possible, just as you should try to speak to an audience of mixed expertise in terms that all members can find stimulating.

When you have successfully married the needs and level of your audience with your stated objectives, you have completed the pre-planning work vital to constructing a good speech. The next stage is to consider presentation and style and the planning of your speech, keeping the audience, its needs and expectations, firmly in mind.

Now read the key points from chapter two overleaf.

KEY POINTS FROM CHAPTER TWO

- The one golden rule when speaking in public is that you should always keep your audience in mind.

- If you address the audience's needs and use language that they understand, then you will go a long way towards a successful speech.

- Each audience can be profiled in terms of its educational background and expertise.

- When you have successfully married the needs and level of your audience with your stated objectives, you have completed the pre-planning work vital to constructing a good speech.

3
DEVELOPING YOUR PRESENTATION SKILLS HINTS ON STYLE

PERSONAL SKILLS

Body Language

People have a natural ability to use body language together with speech. Body language emphasizes speech and enables us to communicate more effectively with others. It is vitally important when preparing for the role of public speaker to understand the nature of your body language and also to connect this to another all important element-*vision*.

Vision

People tend to take in a lot of information with their eyes and obviously presentations are greatly enhanced by use of visual aids. Together, when presenting to a group of people, as a public speaker, *body language and visual stimuli* are all important. A great amount of thought needs to go into the elements of what it is that you are about to present and the way you intend to convey your message. What you should not do, especially as a novice, is to stand up in front of a group and deliver a presentation off the top of your head. You need to carry out thorough research into what it is you are presenting and to whom you are presenting.

Developing a style

Every person engaged in public speaking will have his or her own style. At the one end of the spectrum there are those people who give no thought to what it is they are doing and have no real interest in the audience. For them it is a chore and one that should be gotten over as soon as is possible. Such public speakers can be slow, boring and ineffectual leaving only traces of annoyance in the audience's mind. Here, there is a definite absence of style.

At the other end of the spectrum are those who have given a great deal of thought to what they are doing, given a great deal of thought to their material and have a genuine interest in the audience. Such public speakers will be greatly stimulating and leave a lasting impression and actually convey something of some worth.

It does not matter what the occasion of your public speaking role is, wedding (best mans speech etc.) seminar, presentation to employers. The principles are the same-that is understanding your material, understand the nature of yourself as you relate to the material and how this will translate into spoken and body language and also how you will use visual aids to enhance the presentation.

Underlying all of this is your *own personal style*, partly which develops from an understanding of the above and partly from an understanding of yourself. Some presenters of material recognize their own speed of presentation, i.e. slow, medium or fast and also understand their own body language. Some are more fluent than others, use their hands more etc. Having recognized your own style what you need to do is to adjust your own way of presentation to the specific requirements of the occasion.

The key point is to gain attention, get the message across and be stimulating to a degree. Obviously some occasions are more formal than others. You should study the nature of the occasion and give a lot of thought to what is required, i.e. degree of humor, seriousness etc.

All of the above considerations begin to translate themselves into a style that you yourself will begin to recognize and feel comfortable with. Once this occurs you will find that, when presenting, your nerves will begin to melt away and your confidence begins to develop

Formal presentations

As this is a book about public speaking, with the emphasis on the more formal setting, we should now concentrate on the various elements that go to make up a successful presentation to a group.

There is not one particular style appropriate to public speaking. Each occasion will merit it's own approach. However, there are a few commonly observed rules.

Use of language

The use of language is a specific medium that must be understood when making a presentation. Obviously, if you are speaking publicly to a group of familiar people who know and understand you, a different approach will be needed and a different form of language, perhaps less formal, utilized than that used in front of a group who are totally unfamiliar.

Nevertheless, using formal but simple language interspersed with funny remarks is undoubtedly one of the best ways to approach any form of audience, friends or not. You should certainly avoid too much detail and do not go overboard with funny comments as this will become tedious. Stick to the subject matter lightening up the occasion with a few anecdotes and witty comments. It is all about the right blend and pitch.

Body Language

We have briefly discussed body language. It is astounding how much you can tell about people in the street by simply observing their body language. Usually people form an impression about another within the first five minutes of meeting. It is essential, in a public speaking situation that your body language should reflect a confident personality with a good sense of humor. In order to achieve this you should think about the following:

Use of hands

- Use your hands to emphasize what you say and to invite the audience to accept your point

- Keep your hands open and keep your fingers open.

- Avoid putting your hands in your pocket and avoid closing them. Firmly avoid pointing fingers

- Co-ordinate your hand movements with your words.

Using facial expressions

People tend to concentrate on the face of a public speaker, in addition to the movements of the body. Obviously, your face, along with body language is a vehicle for expression. A smile every now and again is important. There are other actions that can help:

- Use of eyebrows for inviting people to accept your ideas

- Moving the head to look at all members of a group. Very important indeed to maintain a sense of involvement on the part of all

- Do not fix your eyes on one place or person for long. This will isolate the rest of the audience and may be interpreted as nervousness or a lack of confidence on your part

- Look at individuals every time you mention something in their area of expertise or are singling them out in a positive way

- Look at people even if they appear not to be looking at you

The face is a very important part of the communication apparatus and the use of this part of the body is of the utmost importance when public speaking.

Controlling your movements

In addition to the use of face and hands the way you move can have an effect on your audience. Your movements can vary from standing rigid and fixed to acting out roles and being fluid generally. There are in keeping with body language generally, certain rules relating to movement:

- Restrict your movements only to those that are most necessary. Avoid throwing yourself all over the place and distracting peoples attention from the emphasis of your presentation

- Always face the people that you are addressing. Never look at the floor or away from the audience, at least not for a prolonged period of time

Dress

When adopting the role of public speaker it is very important to be dressed formally and in accordance with the standard of the occasion, or the nature of the occasion. Dressing formally does not mean automatically wearing a suit and tie. It does mean however that you should think in terms of power dressing. This means that you wish to make an impression on people, not just through what you say and do, not just through your body language or visual presentations but by the way you look.

People must be impressed. This means that you must give thought to what you wear, how you can help to achieve a sense of control through dress.

Attitude

Your attitude is crucial to your success in public speaking. Attitudes can be greatly influenced by nerves and by being ill prepared. There is nothing worse than a public speaker who slowly degenerates into aggression or hostility through sarcasm or other forms of attack. Yet this is all too frequent. At all times you must maintain a professional and formal attitude that allows you to remain in control. You can think yourself into this state if you find yourself slipping or feel that you are losing control.

If you feel that you are straying in any way then you should get back on course. This can be achieved through a number of ways such as by changing the subject slightly in order to give yourself time to gather your wits or by asking the group to refocus on the subject in question.

Attitude is also disciplined by self-composure that can be engendered through relaxation that in turn is brought about by understanding the role of exercise and meditation, which we will be elaborating on a little later.

Formalities

Another fundamental rule of presentations is the way you open or introduce the presentation and the way you close. When public speaking, it is always necessary to introduce yourself even if most of the audience know who you are. It is vital that everyone knows who you are, who you represent, if anybody, and what you are there for. Having got these necessary formalities over with, the audience will feel more comfortable listening to you because they now have a point of reference.

Depending on the situation, you may even want to ask the audience if they would like to introduce themselves, through a "round robin" which entails each person telling you and the others who they are, and what they hope to get out of the presentation. This approach however, is only really necessary and useful in seminar or teaching situations. Such an approach would be wholly inappropriate in a speech situation.

Practicing presentations

Taking into account all of the above and then practicing. This is the absolute key to successful presentations and to effective public speaking. Practice most certainly lifts your confidence level up and assists you in staying in control The more time and effort that you spend practicing the less that you will have to worry about when presenting. Let's face it, a presentation is a live stage show. How do stand up comic's feel when they expose themselves to an audience? Develop a practicing technique by trying different methods:

- You should choose a topic that you are very interested in and prepare a short presentation on it.

- Stand in front of a mirror and present to yourself. Repeat this over and over observing different aspects of your style.

- Try to rectify any bad habits.

- Experiment with various styles and techniques until you find one that suits you.

- Try to film yourself if possible. Replay the film and observe yourself. This is one of the most effective ways of changing your style, or developing your style.

- Ask a friend to observe you and to make detailed criticism. Do not be afraid of criticism as this is always constructive

At this point you should be concentrating on style only. Do not worry about content as we will be discussing this a little later.

Now read the key points from chapter three.

KEY POINTS FROM CHAPTER THREE

- Body language emphasizes speech and helps us to communicate more effectively with others

- Visual stimuli is equally as important when public speaking

- It is very important to develop your own style as a public speaker

- The use of language is a specific medium which must be understood when public speaking

- Formal but simple language interspersed with funny remarks is one of the best ways to approach an audience

- The use of facial expressions is very important when addressing others

- The way you move can have a very important effect on an audience

- Adopt an appropriate mode of dress for the audience you are addressing. It is better to be smart than scruffy

- Your attitude is crucial to your success as a public speaker

- The way you open and close your presentation is of the utmost importance

- You should always practice presentations before the event

4

EFFECTIVE DELIVERY

In the last chapter, we discussed presentation and style. We also touched on delivery of a speech. In this chapter, we shall further concentrate on delivery.

Good delivery of a speech is a matter of being confident that you can remember what to say, and when and how you want to say it. It is also about communicating with an audience, not only through what you say, but through the attitude of your body, and by the expression of your voice. Good delivery, like a good speaking style, can be learned through adequate rehearsal and control of your nerves.

Presenting a speech

There are several ways to present a speech that you have prepared. Some formal conference occasions, for example, demand that you read your paper verbatim. Even if the form does not demand that the speaker read the speech, you may decide that you want to do so, for safety's sake.

Most speakers, however, decide to forego the security of relying on notes and rely instead on some form of memory jogging notes, or cue cards, to keep them on track. In this way, it is easier to communicate directly with the audience.

Some people have very good memories. If this is the case, you may decide to deliver the speech straight from the heart. Learning a script by heart means that the words are fixed in the brain. Because of this, the speaker will usually find it very difficult to move away from the pattern and introduce new phrases or anecdotes.

You should watch people who are reciting from memory. Their energy and attention is, usually, turned inwards instead of concentrating on the audience. If you are trying to remember what is coming next, you are not going to be able to direct your energies towards the audience. The only people who are really capable of delivering a memorized speech to an audience are trained actors who have had many years experience.

Given this fact, it would pay to consider one of the following alternatives.

Reading your speech

This method will decrease the spontaneity of your speech. The speaker is tied to the script and less able to ad lib. Reading from a script also reduces the opportunity you have to make eye contact with the audience, and to register their reaction to what you are saying.

There are several circumstances when you might want to read from a script, however. You may be addressing an academic conference where it is necessary to read from a prepared paper. You may also be involved in a complex audio-visual presentation. In this case, the script may have to be annotated in line with the presentation.

In the first case, the language employed to write the paper is likely to be fairly formal, constrained as you are by the academic environment. You can add some interest to the presentation by adding some personal (short) anecdotes or illustrations not used in the original paper. If you are totally constrained then you should try making the script as conversational as possible.

If you do intend to read from a script, type it on a word processor using larger font than normal. Double-space it and finish a sentence at the bottom of the page not start a page mid-sentence. This will interrupt your flow. Make sure that you number the pages and use firm, not flimsy, paper.

A third circumstance where you might find yourself reading from a prepared script is if you are giving a political or business speech. These type of speeches are usually prepared by a professional speech-writer and they are using carefully selected quotes that cannot be construed. To avoid such a presentation sounding like nothing more than a carefully prepared statement, make sure that you have time to rehearse fully. Try to become very familiar with the speech so that it is delivered more naturally on the day. Make sure that you have understood the essence of the speech.

Delivering a speech from a script will probably be a requirement thrust upon you by circumstance. Or, if you are inexperienced, you may need this for safety. However, it is usually best, if you are trying to communicate properly with an audience, to read and use notes to provide a cue.

Abbreviating your script

The most effective method of delivering a script of almost any kind is to abbreviate the script to a series of key words that can be written on a sheet of paper or blank cue cards that can more easily be held in a shaking hand.

The advantage of this system is that because you are not being spoon fed with the actual words of your script, you are free to extemporize, to go in search of fresh words and phrases. Because you are only reading key words rather than whole sentences, your eyes are free to roam the room, make eye contact with members of the audience, and you are likely to be able to better gauge their attitude to what you are saying.

Physically, cue cards or sheets are a lot more wieldy than full scripts. The effect of this is to signal to the audience that you are relaxed. You can also use your arms and hands more freely to communicate.

Most of all, working from brief notes gives you the freedom to think on your feet, while giving you the security of knowing that, if you lose your way, you will only have to glance at your cue to find your way again.

Cue cards or notes will be annotations of a full script and as such, you will have to prepare them from this. You should go through your speech and highlight key words or ideas and write on to your cue cards or sheets each of these words under the appropriate heading or sub heading. Include one-word memory joggers to cue the use of visual aids.

Obviously, the only way cue cards or sheets are going to work on the day is by practicing them. Therefore, ensure that you keep practicing until you are very confident of the whole speech and that the entirety is lodged in your mind. In this way, it does not matter how nervous you are on the day, you have both your notes and your memory to revert to.

In person

Human methods of communication do not rely solely on words. People are watching each other constantly for physical clues as to what the other is feeling or thinking. Equally, tone of voice conveys a lot. Taking control of these two methods of communication is very important indeed.

First impressions

As discussed earlier, when you first move into a person's field of vision, they make an instant judgement on your appearance. The same thing happens when you first move in front of an audience. The style of your dress will mark you out, whether you are smartly dressed or whether you are casual or wearing a particular mode of dress that puts you into a particular slot, dress has a 'tribal' effect and people will categorize you on the spot.

Take advantage of these common perceptions in order to put the audience in the right frame of mind to listen to your speech. Be smartly dressed and avoid wearing anything that is outlandish. Pay attention to detail. Do not overdress. This can also distract your audience from your material.

Posture and movement

The second element of your appearance that your audience will detect at first sight is that of your posture, the way you move. As with many animals, your posture and movement will send strong signals about you as a person and also about your attitude to the people you are with. For example, stooping and bowing your head indicates uncertainty and that we are unsure of our ground. Holding the head up high indicates confidence and security.

From the moment you face your audience, make sure you pay attention to your posture. Hold your shoulders square, head high and avoid slouching. Sit towards the front of a chair, rather than sitting back. Do not cross your legs at the knee. Try to convey the impression that you are relaxed but alert.

When you talk, do so with purpose. Always speak on your feet and fix your eyes on the audience. Stand upright, do not slouch. Place your feet a few inches apart with the weight on the balls rather than on the heels of the feet. This means that your body is balanced and that you are leaning towards the audience slightly.

From this basic speaking position, you should be able to move in a relaxed yet purposeful manner. Avoid shuffling around.

Eye contact

It would be useful to watch an actor when they are making eye contact and to try to work out what it is they are doing with their eyes. In most cases, the actor is doing his or her level best to avoid looking into the eyes of another person.

By making eye contact, we are expressing our openness towards other people. We are also showing that we are not frightened of them and that we are interested in their feelings, thoughts and reactions. When the contact is made, a direct line of communication is opened up and the listener's attention is held.

Making eye contact with an audience is one of the most valuable skills that a speaker can learn. Eye contact can be practiced in almost any social situation, and you will be surprised how it changes people's reaction to you. They will become more attentive and more willing to trust what it is you have to say. They will begin to look upon you as a more approachable person-exactly the kind of response that you want from your audience.

When you are speaking to a group, avoid picking out one single member of the audience and making eye contact exclusively with him or her. This will make that person very uncomfortable and the rest of the audience will begin to feel excluded. Make eye contact with different individuals round the room so that you take in the whole audience.

If you are inexperienced and nervous, you may not wish to make eye contact straight away. In this case, deliver your first couple of lines to a point above the audience's head. However, as soon a the time is appropriate, start making eye contact. This should come as you feel more confident.

You will find that if you have opted to read your speech from a script, you will find it very difficult to make time to make eye contact. Eye contact is central to delivering your message in a personal and effective way and, for this reason, it is important to free your eyes from the written word.

If you cannot perfect the art of making eye contact with your audience then you will probably find that your speech-making efforts are doomed to failure.

Hand gestures

As with body movement, hand gestures can add to, rather than detract from, the spoken word. They should be produced as part of your enthusiasm for and knowledge of your subject. If you are speaking to a foreign audience, make sure that you know what you are doing and what your gestures mean, as certain movements that may be innocent and acceptable to the west, may be unacceptable to those from the Middle East, for example.

You should watch how others use gesture in everyday conversations, such as pointing, stabbing, clenching the fist and so on. There are two things to avoid when it comes to hand gestures. First, beware of fidgeting, this can be irritating. Second, try not to make too many meaningless gestures as these may confuse the audience. Do not, for example, keep waving your arms around for emphasis.

Facial expression

The golden rule on facial expression is: smile, but not too much. A smile means that you are friendly, are happy to be there and are relaxed. However, try not too smile fixedly through thick and thin, allowing no other response to register on your face. People will mistrust you and see you as behaving unnaturally.

Voice control

The third element in delivering a speech is your voice. Good vocal delivery can be broken down into two factors: volume-speaking to be heard; expression-speaking to be understood. The basic skill in voice control is breathing. (See voice control)

Expression

The way a speaker expresses his or her words adds to their meaning in much the same way as hand gestures. Expression involves three elements: pitch variation-the tone of your voice; pace-the speed at which you speak; and phrasing-sculpting your phrases into a meaningful form. Rehearsal with a tape recorder should enable you to pinpoint faults in your expression.

Pitch

As a rule, younger people tend to have higher pitched voices than older people. It follows that, because older people are considered to have more authority than younger people, those with lower voices are thought of in the same way. Emotional state can also determine pitch, nervousness being characterized by higher pitch for example.

Some teachers of public speaking advocate that you work towards a lower tone for these reasons. However, if one of the keys to good delivery is being natural then this may not be a good idea. For the majority of people, controlled breathing and careful phrasing should automatically improve the tone of voice.

Pace

It is important to ensure that the pace of your speech is measured. You must give your audience time to hear and assimilate the words you are saying, and yourself time to think where the next sentence is coming from. Slower than normal speech also indicates that you have something important to say.

As you work with your speech, add indications of pauses of different lengths. These will help you to add emphasis. Slowing speech can also give you time to improve your diction.

Phrasing

The words you have written out in a full script fall into small groups-perhaps sentences or parts of sentences (individual clauses). To better communicate the meaning of each of these groups of words, you need to take each one as an individual unit and try to imbue it with the single meaning that it contains.

Different meanings require different 'shapes'. A question, for example, should be spoken with an upturn at the end. Without the upturn, the question could be taken as a statement.

Using a microphone

In general, try to avoid using a microphone-it can make the voice sound unnatural and hinders the task of appearing to be conversational. It may, however, be unavoidable in certain circumstances, to use a microphone, open air meetings and so on. You should always check with the organizers of the event whether they expect you to use a microphone. Try the microphone out and make sure that all can hear you, particularly those at the rear. If you have to use a microphone, it is best to practice, probably at home. You must get your voice to the right volume and you must find out how far away from the microphone you can move before your voice gets lost. Teach yourself to avoid feedback at all costs as this can severely distract the audience.

Presenting visual aids

If you have incorporated any form of visual aid into your presentation, you will need to pay particular attention to your body language. Your first consideration should be to not allow the visual aid to come between you and your audience.

Too many speakers bend down and read overhead transparencies, or turn their backs on the audience to see which slide comes next. However great the temptation to do otherwise, always speak to the audience, and not to the equipment. You will help yourself if you make it a rule never to operate the visual equipment whilst speaking.

The second problem with presenting visual aids is that they present untold opportunities for nervous speakers to fiddle. If you have to change a transparency or reveal an exhibit, do so with as little extra movement as possible. Make sure that before you start speaking, your transparencies are in order and if you need something to point with it is to hand.

Time for rehearsal

Skilful use of equipment such as microphones and visual aids can be learned through practice and familiarity. In the same way, all the techniques that combine to make a good delivery-effective use of notes, understanding and controlling the body and voice-can be assimilated through rehearsal until they are second nature.

It is therefore essential, especially if speaking in public is a new experience, that you devote some time to rehearsing. Depending on your schedule, you may have a little or a lot of time to rehearse. Rehearsals need not take a long time, possibly an hour or so every session, depending on the length of the speech. You should allow enough time before the actual speech to fit enough practice sessions in.

What to look for in rehearsal

There are several stages in a progressive rehearsal of a speech. You may begin with the full script of the speech in front of you, or notes, and you may intend to simply read from the script on the day or to produce it as notes. Here are some suggestions what to look out for at each stage. Whatever stage you are at, it is always a good idea to stand up and try to deliver the speech to an imaginary audience. It is also a good idea to rehearse with your visual aids right from the start.

1. At the first stage, you are either working from notes or from an annotated script. Read through. Try out alternative phrases and descriptions, add pauses, and try to decide whether your speech hangs together as a logical and coherent train of thought. Note down any changes, and try the whole thing again. It may take a number of read-throughs before you are happy with your speech.

Ask yourself these questions:

- Is this speech about the topic that I have chosen?

- Is there anything superfluous that I can cut out?

- Is this speech appropriate to the audience and the occasion?

- Am I using the right visuals for the right reasons?

- Is this speech likely to help me achieve my objectives?

Time your speech. Make sure that it is shorter than the time limit you have been given-you need to leave time for audience reaction. Make any cuts necessary to ensure that you do not run over time. If you run short, you can always fill in by taking questions. However, do not run over, this is not acceptable.

When you are certain that the material and the basic form of your speech are right, transfer it to cue cards, or whichever form of notes that you have chosen. If you are already working from notes, it would be a good idea to rewrite them, to take account of the changes that you have made. If you intend to work from the script, it might be a good idea to rewrite it.

2. From this point on, try not to add anything to your notes or script. Run through the speech a couple of times more. If you have picked out a couple of sentences that you would like to learn by heart, do it now. Keep experimenting with new words and phrases. Work hard to draw out each thought into a full picture of what you mean to say. Vary the pitch, pace and volume of your voice. If it helps, you should rehearse in a quiet room Away from distractions.

3. At this stage, you might like to record your speech, so that you can analyze the oral element of your delivery. Do not play back straight

away, leave it an hour or so then you will come to it with a fresh mind. Listen hard and ask yourself the following questions:

- Are you speaking slowly enough?

- Are you varying the pace slightly?

- Are you making good use of pauses?

- Do your sentences turn down at the ends?

- Are you giving the right kinds of expression to your words?

- Are there places where you are having difficulty expressing yourself?

- Do you use fillers: er, um, you know, you see and so on?

Check the timing again-it is very easy to over elaborate once you are familiar with your material. Run through a couple more times, trying out remedies to the faults that you have detected.

4. Next, draft in a friend who is able to take in the whole experience of your delivery-your appearance and message as well as your voice. Ask him or her to be objective and constructive in their criticisms. As you deliver your speech again, imagine that your friend is in the middle of a whole group of people and practice making eye contact with the audience.

Ensure that no punches are pulled in this encounter with your friend as it is vital that you finally polish up your speech and your method of delivery. Remember, at this stage, the time is drawing close for you to stand up and present your speech. It must be as perfect as possible before the day.

Now read the key points from chapter 4

KEY POINTS FROM CHAPTER FOUR

- Good delivery of a speech is a matter of being confident that you can remember what to say, and when and how you want to say it.

- Most speakers forego the security of notes and use cue cards as an aid to effective delivery.

- The most effective method of delivering a script of almost any kind is to abbreviate the script to a series of key words.

- Whichever way you decide to deliver a speech, ensure that you have practiced thoroughly.

- The style of your dress will mark you out and people will categorize you on the spot.

- Audiences will pick up on the way that you move.

- Audiences will also pick up on eye contact, hand gestures and facial expressions.

- Control of the voice is very important when delivering a speech.

- Adequate rehearsals are very important indeed before delivering a speech.

5

PREPARATION OF MATERIALS

Carrying out effective research

Having considered some of the personal skills needed in order to become an effective public speaker, we now need to concentrate on the nature of the material used. Remember, the most important elements of public speaking are the person delivering the speech/presentation and the material.

When you are faced with the task of public speaking, which involves presentation of material, any material, then the first point to be aware of is that you will need to carry out some sort of research. Although you may feel fairly well versed in the area in question, it is always advisable to do a little research. This counts for speeches at a wedding as well as more complex presentations in front of a group of people.

There are certain fundamental questions that should be asked before researching any topic. The first one is, how much do you know about the topic and who are you presenting to? How long are you presenting for and when and where is the presentation taking place?

Gathering information/identification of sources

Gathering information can be time consuming and requires effort. However, if you wish to ensure that you have quality information relevant to the topic in hand then this cannot be avoided. Start by identifying the topics that you are covering and work out various ways of getting appropriate materials. Once you know what you need then you need to carry out checks on the different locations, i.e., libraries, universities etc.

You need to ensure that you have effective ways of storing data. This is quite important and there are several key ways of ensuring that you stay organized:

- File the information that you have researched and index the file

- If you have ready access to a computer, save any information on the database and create easy to follow search fields

- Use key search words to classify the information, and divide each file into sub-files.

Any of the above are suitable for organizing your information, manual or computerized. The most important thing is to be able to retrieve it readily.

Filtering and assembling the information

Once you feel that you have enough information then you have to decide how much of it you want to use. Great care should be taken to ensure that your material is to the point, covers all angles, but is not over laden with unnecessary facts.

Once you have decided what topics the presentation is going to include, it is important to put it into words that you can remember, or feel comfortable with when you are giving your talk. Getting started is always difficult. The introduction to a speech or presentation is the most difficult part and it is the point where you may be overtaken by nerves. It is worth leaving this part of your speech or presentation to the end so that you have worked through the main body and can then assemble a knowledgeable beginning. Do not try to achieve perfection with your presentation or you may end up a bag of nerves and end up spending more time than you had anticipated without really achieving the desired end.

You should always prepare a script in the first instance. It could be that you wish to memorize the material and deliver an off the cuff presentation to your audience. However, it is always advisable to write a script. Having a script, or a crib sheet as a framework helps you avoid the dangers of trying to improvise which can lead you into a corner and undermine your confidence if you lose track of what you are saying. Ideally, your level of comfort with the content of your presentation should be the sum of your level of knowledge of the subject and the level of your preparation.

The script writing process

The following is one way of preparing a script that is effective but simple.

Preparing a first draft

- Start developing your ideas into a short story

- Rely on your memory to start with to see what you can put together without referring to your notes. This helps you clarify your ideas and find out how much you know about the subject.

- Avoid expressing yourself in a negative way and use positive terms whenever you can.

- Using factual language reflects a friendly and convincing tone. Extravagant expressions can only serve to confuse the listener.

Dealing with excessive information

An important factor that may affect the length of your script is the time that you have available to you. It is very important to keep to the time allowed. One of the major contributors to nerves is overrunning the length of time that you have.

One of the most common problems with report style presentations is to include a large amount of information, within a short time, which can be very confusing to the audience. If your script is obviously too long, edit it by removing details and leaving highlights of the important points. Conversely, you may find that you do not have enough material to present. One of the most common solutions here, again within a report style presentation is to ask questions of the audience to fill in time.

The final draft

When all these changes are complete, you will have a final draft of your presentation. It is now up to you to learn to deliver it as a speech or talk. Whatever you try to do, try to be as natural as you possibly can. If you are making a formal presentation then try to use graphic illustrations to ensure that the message is getting home. Obviously, if you are making a speech at a wedding then this is inappropriate. As we discussed in chapter four, when you have written your speech you should, preferably, reduce this to a series of cue cards. This will help in the final delivery of your speech.

Now read the key points from Chapter five

KEY POINTS FROM CHAPTER FIVE

- It is necessary to carry out research into any material that you intend to present in public

- Start by identifying the topics that you will be covering and work out various ways of getting appropriate materials

- You need effective ways of storing and retrieving data

- You should always prepare a script in the first instance

- After preparing a script, you will need to learn to deliver it as a talk

- Before delivering your talk or speech, it will be necessary to carry out some planning

- You will need to put your ideas into sequence

6

VISUAL AIDS

Before we further discuss presentation of your material it is necessary to talk a little about the use of visual aids.

Visual aids are used for effect, for helping you to make your point. They offer audiences a visual representation of what you are trying to put across. Generally, you can explain a point much quicker with the use of visual aids.

Visual aids also keep audiences interested, as there is more entertainment value with the use of visual images than there is with the spoken word. Combined with words, visual aids help you to communicate ideas in a very short time and leave a longer lasting impression on the audience.

This is only true, though, if you use them to their best effect. The opposite can have a detrimental effect on the audience.

Visual aids are not effective if they are not prepared very carefully together with the script that you are presenting. Do not try to overload the visual aid in terms of its contents or this will, more often than not, confuse your audience.

Whether you use a graph, diagram or picture on the slide (if it is a slide that you are using) then put only one on each slide. When working on the main body of the slide keep the following in mind:

- Keep it as simple as possible

- Use pictures as often as you can keeping text to a minimum

- Leave plenty of space between items for visibility

- Use professional images (computer generated) as opposed to hand drawn.

Presenting with visual images

Images are there to help you and you should be comfortable with using the equipment that displays them. The following tips are useful when presenting:

- Ignore the existence of a picture behind you. Never turn your back on the audience. Talk to them at the same time as they are looking at the image
- Always rehearse with your visual aids. This will help you to familiarize yourself with the equipment and also to remember the sequence in which you will present the slides
- If you are going to use an overhead projector, make sure that all your acetates are in order. Put them back in the same order when you finish so that they are ready for use the next time. Keep them clean.
- Stand to one side of the overhead projector when you are presenting. Use a pointer to make a relevant point. Let the audience see where you are pointing your pointer.

Tools for the presentation of visual aids

Use of an Overhead projector

This particular tool is the most popular of all visual aids. It is widely used in all forms of presentations because of its flexibility. It can be used to project almost any form of material.

Slide projectors

This is the second most popular tool for visual aids The quality is always very good, often much better than the OHP. However, it can be more expensive to produce materials than the OHP.

Using a video

This is the most effective visual aid but should be used only for limited periods. More information can be shown in a short space of time than other forms of visual aid.

Use of a monitor view pad

This is a relatively new method of projection. The device has a transparent liquid display screen which, when connected to a computer acts as a monitor. The screen can then be placed on an OHP to replace an acetate.

This is slightly more technical and long-winded than the OHP on its own but the results can be very professional.

Use of other visual aids

In addition to the main method chosen by yourself there are other peripheral visual aids that you may wish to utilize. The following are also quite effective:

- *Flip chart.* This particular tool enables you to write and draw as you go along. Also very useful if you wish people to break into groups in order to carry out an exercise.

- *models and prototypes.* Showing a model is very powerful when trying to demonstrate a particular point. Displaying models of buildings can be more effective than showing plans.

Use of color

Color is also a very powerful medium when you wish to make important information stand out. The audience can focus on the colored parts with the background information remaining in the background.

Working with computers

Computers are playing an increasingly important part in presentations. Whether you are making or presenting slides, the results look more professional and effective with the use of presentation or graphics software.

Choosing the right equipment

It is important to use the right kind of visual aids for each occasion. If used incorrectly, visual aids can give the wrong impression or even ruin your chances of success in getting your message across. Choosing the right visual aid is quite difficult. The following are points to consider:

- The ability to grab the audience's attention. There is no point in using the most impressive equipment if it will not appeal to the audience

- The suitability for the occasion. You do not need to use state of the art equipment if you are giving a short speech. Use the most appropriate form of equipment

- The effect of your visual aids on the audience. Will the visual aid that you intend to use help or just confuse the audience. You should very carefully ensure that what you use perfectly compliments your presentation.

Use of notes and handouts

It is sometimes useful to provide your audience with a handout of your presentation, or part of your presentation. This very much depends on what you are presenting. Only provide handouts when needed and not at the start of the presentation as this will distract the audience from what it is you are trying to say and also the content of any visual aid.

Involving the audience

Sometimes you may wish to involve the audience in an interactive presentation. If you need to make a quick survey or opinion poll to prove a point, you can pass a short questionnaire to the audience and let someone help you in counting the votes and presenting.

Always remember, visual aids are there to assist you in presenting your message and if they don't achieve that don't bother with them.

Now read the key points from chapter Six

KEY POINTS FROM CHAPTER SIX

- Visual aids are for effect, for helping you to make your point

- Visual aids are not effective if they are not prepared in line with the material that you are presenting

- Keep visual aids as simple as possible

- Use professional images

- When presenting, stand to one side to enable the audience to see what it is that you are presenting

- Select carefully the tool for presenting the visual aids

- The use of notes and handouts can be important in some cases

7

USING THE VOICE IN DELIVERY

We now need to consider one of the most important aspects of public speaking, the voice.

What you say is very important indeed. However, even more important is the way that you say it. The right combination of body language and voice is far more potent than a clever and witty script. The two combined can help you become a very effective public speaker indeed.

The voice

The voice plays a very important role in presentation and public speaking generally. The way you pitch your voice is guaranteed to either keep peoples attention or send them to sleep.

The voice is a result of air coming out of your lungs that causes the vocal chords to vibrate, producing different sounds. These various sounds are shaped into words by the speech organism in the head.

The brain then sends messages controlling the breathing and the tension of the vocal chords. Cavities in the body, such as the mouth and chest, provide amplification. The amplified sounds are then shaped into recognizable speech by the tongue, lips teeth etc. Speech is produced in two different ways:

- Voiced sounds-produced by speech organs in the mouth closer to the vocal chords at the back end of the tongue

- Unvoiced sounds-produced mainly using the tongue and front teeth. The sound of the letter S is produced in this way.

All the above aspects of voice and speech are controlled by the body organs that are unique to each person. We can develop the ability to control these organs to produce the speech that we want. This can be achieved by training the various muscles that produce and shape sounds. The shape of various cavities, such as the chest, can be changed to vary the level of sound amplification.

Developing your voice

It is perfectly possible, and probably essential to improve on four characteristics of your speech:

- tone

- pitch

- volume

- clarity.

Tone

If you restrict your body cavities responsible for amplifying sound, your voice will sound restricted and sometimes nasal. Restriction of body cavities can happen by standing or sitting in the wrong way. *It is essential that you give thought to your posture and bearing when public speaking.*

Pitch

As you stretch and loosen your voice chords, the pitch of your voice will change. When stretched, the number of vibrations increases due to the small distance allowed for them to vibrate. These vibrations produce high frequency (pitch) sounds. When the vocal chords are loose, more distance is allowed for them to vibrate which makes them produce low frequency (pitch) sounds.

Volume

The volume of your voice can be improved in two ways. The first is by simply increasing the pressure of air coming out of your lungs, or by narrowing the space between the vocal chords (glottis). You can change the volume of a whisper simply by increasing the amount of air through your glottis that is widely open. Try to shout. You will notice that your glottis contracts sharply, to increase the volume of your voice.

Clarity

To get your message across you need to say it clearly. Clarity is determined by the speech organs and how well you can control them. If you are too nervous your tongue and lips start playing tricks on you because they are tense. In order to speak clearly, overcome the problems associated with speech organs and get your message across.

Don't be scared of moving your lips. Exercise your speech muscles. Make sure that you pronounce things clearly and that you carry your voice.

Voice pitch

People generally feel more comfortable listening to a deep voice, one that is well rounded and smooth. However, it is important to ensure that your voice is at your natural pitch and not forced. To find your natural pitch, concentrate on the following exercises:

- Speak at the lowest note that feels comfortable to you

- Use a musical instrument, e.g. a guitar or piano and find the note that corresponds to your lowest comfortable pitch

- Move four notes up the musical scale. This should be very close to your natural pitch

- Try to tune your voice with this note and speak with the music helping you to stay in tune

- Practice this as many times as you need, in order to become confident in finding your natural pitch quite quickly.

When you have found the natural pitch of your voice, you will need to work on some variations to make your speech more natural. Changing the pitch up and down according to the contents of the speech helps you to keep the audience attracted to what you are saying. Try saying a few sentences out loud and practice varying the pitch. You can then notice the relation between the contents of the sentences and your pitch when saying each of them. When you realize what you are capable of achieving with your voice, you can then consciously start varying the pitch.

Singing is very good for voice training and realizing the potential of your voice organs. Reading out loud and trying to act a story is also good training.

Use of silences and pauses

Sometimes, silence can be more effective than words. It is useful to pause every now and again to allow the listeners to absorb the ideas that you have put across. A short pause gives the audience time to absorb what you have said. You can also use pauses to help you relax and breath. Pauses also help you put your ideas together to start elaborating on a new point.

A few useful hints on the use of pauses:

- Don't feel compelled to fill the silence. If you find yourself speaking quickly for no real reason, force yourself to pause. Sometimes you may be very enthusiastic about what you are saying and find yourself speaking rapidly. Pause and use your body language and voice to show your enthusiasm

- Avoid becoming a slow speaker. Moderate the speed of your talk to the level of its contents. Always remember that the aim is to be understood and not to say as many words as possible within the given time

- Try to maintain the rhythm and the rate of flow of ideas throughout your presentation. Again this can be achieved by practicing your presentation enough times to make you feel confident and in command.

Emphasis

There are other ways to emphasize a point or an idea. The amount of stress put on a syllable can also emphasize the word. You should say certain sentences, placing emphasis on different words. A few examples are:

- Can I have that *chair* please

- Can I have *that* chair please

In the first sentence you are asking for the chair and not something else. In the second sentence, you want the chair to be given to you and not someone else. Therefore, placing the stress on a word can change the whole sentence.

Avoid putting emphasis on too many words. This diminishes the effect of the technique and renders it useless.

It is important to realize that emphasis in many cases is placed on a group of words rather than just one. The same technique applies, but in the case of a group of words, the pitch change to the decisive tone can be extended to include all the words in the group. The whole group should be treated as one entity with the emphasis on the group and not the individual words.

Voice projection

Voice projection depends on two main factors:

- Physical

- Psychological

The physical factor comprises

- The force with which you breathe

- The muscular power you put into forming the words

- The clarity of your pronunciation

If you get all these factors right then you will have no problem in projecting your voice. However, some people feel nervous in front of an audience and they fail to project their voice properly. In a lot of cases, speakers project their voices too much or too little simply because they do not look at the audience and estimate the power that they need to project.

In order to estimate projection, you should look at the person the furthest away from you and imagine that you are talking too him or her. You will feel the need to project your voice to that person and be able to control your vocal organs and breathing accordingly.

Use of the body

To help you to project your voice, you should make use of the resonance of your body cavities. Try the following:

- Relax the muscles in your neck and stand comfortably without bending or over straightening your chest.

- Also relax the muscles in your neck by nodding gently a few times.

- Take a deep breath and exhale, letting out a deep sound. You can then realize how the cavity in your chest resonates giving out a sigh of relief.

The nose

A clear nose helps you to speak clearly and project your voice. If your nose is blocked, it is harder for you to pronounce certain letters let alone project your voice. It is also easier to breathe through a clear nose and therefore maintain the breathing rhythm.

Improving posture

Other cavities in the body, such as the chest, can be used to create more resonance. It helps if your posture is right. For a good posture try the following:

Relax your muscles especially around the shoulder area. To do so you need to raise your shoulders and drop them a few times.

- Do not bend forward as you speak. This prevents your chest cavity from resonating

- If you stand with a curved back and too stiff you will not be able to project your voice properly
- Relax your body and stand in a natural position. This will help you not only project your voice but maintain it for a longer time too.

Training and looking after your voice

To change your speech habits that you have developed over a number of years, is not a simple matter. You need to consciously work at this before the changes become second nature to you. You should always look after your voice in order to maintain it:

- Avoid smoky rooms

- Allow your voice to rest. Even when you are giving a long talk or speech, you can still rest your voice by regular breathing and proper articulation

- Avoid warm and dry rooms which can bring on a sore throat

- Don't eat dairy products before your presentation, because the production of mucus is increased which roughens the voice

- If you feel that you have a dry mouth and throat, bite your tongue gently. This will produce enough saliva to wet your mouth.

- After a long talk, practice a few relaxing exercises to prepare your voice for rest. These exercises can be stretching, breathing articulation etc.

Now read the key points from chapter seven

KEY POINTS FROM CHAPTER SEVEN

- The voice plays a very important role in presentation and public speaking generally.

- It is possible, and usually essential to improve on the characteristics of your speech.

- Tone, pitch, volume, clarity, the use of silences and pauses, emphasis and voice projection are all essential characteristics of speech.

- You should make an effort to train and take care of your voice.

8

A FEW HINTS ON SETTING

By now, you should have gained a reasonably clear idea of the ground work that you must do before you are ready to stand in front of others and make an effective presentation. In addition, you will have gained some idea of the importance of physical exercise and its relation to your own well-being. However, before you do begin your presentation it will do no harm in considering the type of environment that you will present in.

Choosing the right setting

There are a number of types of place where you may find yourself giving a presentation. These can vary from a small over ventilated room to a large and comfortable seminar room. For a good setting a room should possess the following:

- It should be large enough to accommodate all present

- The temperature should be just right and not uncomfortable (too hot or too warm)

- All seats should be positioned correctly

- Enough space should be provided for visual aids

- Lighting should be controllable

- There should be enough power points close to the location of your equipment

- The acoustics should be suitable.

If you have the chance to go into a room some time before the presentation, look out for aspects which can be improved upon and which bring the room in line with the above criteria.

Further tips are:

- close any windows which overlook a busy street, to avoid noise pollution in the room. If the room is too warm and you need to open a window, do so before the presentation and close them just before you start

- If the room is small, with an elevated platform for the presenter to stand on, arrange the seating to give you enough space in front of the platform. Use this space and avoid standing at a higher level than your small audience. This can only intimidate them and create barriers

- If you can rearrange the seating in the room, always try to place the seats facing you with their back to the room door. This enables latecomers to sneak in without distracting peoples attention from you

- In large lecture theaters, make sure that the lighting is controlled, so that when you start your presentation, it is dimmed in the audience section. This helps the audience focus on you and your visual aids.

- However, it should not be too dark for the audience to take notes if necessary.

9
DEALING WITH NERVES

We discussed public speaking and nervousness at the beginning of this book. However, now that the big day has approached, you may be feeling more nervous than ever. Therefore, it is necessary to look at nerves in more detail.

Fear need not become an obstacle to your success as a speaker. In fact, nervousness can become a positive aid to you ability to put across your message, as long as you learn to take control of it.

Perseverance in the face of fear

In moments of panic it might be difficult to remember why it ever occurred to you to speak in public. Thousands of people stand up in front of audiences every day. Each of these individuals has a different reason for doing it-teachers, sales people, lawyers and so on-the list is endless. When they go out and address their audience they are fulfilling their own and their audiences needs. Learning the skills to be a successful public speaker has many advantages:

- You become more effective in your workplace

- You are better able to recall important facts and figures.

- You are better equipped to research information.

- You become more widely knowledgeable as a result of keeping a close eye on the media.

- You are better able to argue your point.

- You are better able to communicate with people on many different levels.

- You can improve your interview or selling technique.

- You may find that other people consider you more interesting and seek out your company more often.

- You may have the opportunity to pass on your interest in a subject to other people.

- You may be able to persuade people to a good cause.

- You may find yourself making people laugh-one of the greatest gifts of all.

Whatever your reason, remember it when you are beset by nerves. If you have a good enough reason to speak in public, you will succeed in fulfilling your audiences needs and your own.

Fear of public speaking

The best way to describe how a person feels when they are frightened is to list a number of symptoms: sweating, blushing, racing pulse, clumsiness or shaking limbs and a blank mind. The key to fighting debilitating fear is to think beyond the symptoms to the cause.

When asked to list reasons why they may feel fear when faced with speaking in public, the following are often listed as reasons:

- I am inexperienced

- I do not know enough about the subject.

- I am afraid of the audience.

- My mind may go blank.

- The equipment may go wrong.

- I may make a complete fool of myself by saying or doing something stupid.

All of these worries are founded on one fear: the fear of the unknown.

As a novice speaker, making your debut, you may consider yourself in a particularly frightening situation. However, every speaker you have ever heard once made a maiden speech. The fear of the novice quickly disintegrates as soon as that maiden speech is over, so you might as well take the bull by the horns and do it now.

What else is there in the speaking situation that is unknown, and therefore to be feared? You may feel that you do not know your subject well enough, or that you may lose your thread half way through or that your mind will go blank. It is in your power to get rid of this fear by thorough preparation.

If you are not sure of your subject, take action to change it. You may be able to do this by narrowing the field by covering only those subjects of which you are certain. If you think that you might lose your way, take time to rehearse well in advance, so that you can extemporize with ease. Extemporization is merely elaborating a theme. If you know your subject well enough, if you have planned your speech logically, and if you have made good memory jogging notes, you should have no fear of not finding your way back to the right path should you stray for a moment.

Equally, there is no excuse for the fear that your equipment might fail you. Familiarity with the equipment you intend to use, and thorough checking of that available at the venue should put your mind at rest. If you feel terror at the thought of your audience, usually the biggest fear, you should remember that your audience is looking forward to hearing you, they would like to hear you speak and they are expecting you to fulfil at least one of their needs. If you are truly sure of your subject matter then you can speak to any audience with confidence.

Remember, you are the one in charge, you are the one who has control and will deliver a speech that others will enjoy and remember. This is the attitude that you should have, not over confident but just right-at ease and relaxed, comfortable with yourself, and in command of your subject matter.

Relate the art of public speaking to that of an everyday conversation. Very rarely do you lose control of an everyday conversation. There is no reason why you should think any differently of public speaking.

Practical ways of controlling fear

Fear is merely the product of lack of preparation. However, fear is not a rational sentiment, it is a physical response and, try as you might, you cannot banish it. An alternative way of tackling anxiety is through the body, rather than through the brain. People are more prone to anxiety in certain circumstances, and if you can avoid those circumstances then it is possible to reduce stress significantly.

General health

Because fear is a physical reaction, people often find that, when they are feeling below par, they become anxious about trivial things. In the days before your speech, rest and eat properly and keep off alcohol. Take a couple of brisk walks.

Try to avoid stimulants such as caffeine, cigarettes, etc. Try to relax naturally and learn a good breathing exercise.

In seeking to reduce your anxiety, it is not necessary to eradicate it altogether. A taste of nerves keeps your mind alert. It is important to stay on your mettle if you are to appear at your best.

Most of all-remember that you have very little to lose and a lot to gain by speaking in public.

10
DELIVERING YOUR PRESENTATION

On the day

All of your preparation has been leading towards one particular day, that of the event in which you are to speak. The following advice is aimed at reducing the possibility that something might go wrong, and at giving you the chance to control your nerves and perform to the best of your ability.

You are at the point where your speech has been written and your visual and other aids have been prepared. You have also acquired knowledge about your personal self and also you're setting. If possible, you should allow yourself time for a dress rehearsal prior to delivering your speech. Of course, a dress rehearsal may not be necessary on all occasions. However, if you are speaking in front of a lot of people then you may want to at least spend some time taking in the area you will speak in and also to run through a few motions.

Confirmation

In the week before the event, contact the organizers to confirm that all the details supplied to you are correct, and that nothing has changed:

- Name and address of the venue.

- Travel arrangements: parking space; street directions, who, if anyone, will be meeting you at the station?

- Contact name and telephone number should you be held up on the way.

- Time of event-morning or evening?

- Dress requirements.

- Length of speech.

- Names of those to be mentioned in toasts.

- Special facilities if you are disabled.

Do not be put off or fobbed off by harassed organizers who would simply tell you that nothing has changed since the last time you spoke. Make sure that the information is repeated over the phone. If not, have it written down and e-mailed or faxed to you. You must also confirm in writing the arrangements that have been agreed regarding a fee and payment of expenses. Find out who is going to pay you, and where you should send receipts and invoice. Find out also when you can be expected to get paid.

If you are taking large pieces of equipment with you to the venue, and you expect that you will need someone to help you to carry this is and set it up, arrange this before with the organizers.

At the same time that you confirm, put some thought into what you are going to wear. Preparing clothes the night before will lead to trouble. At the same time, ensure that your car is reliable enough to get you to the event or that you know what the public transport arrangements are.

On the eve

Apart from the moments when you arise from your feet to speak, the evening before can be the most stressful time as you anticipate the possible horrors of the following day.

Many people leave their final checks till the day of the speech. It is a good idea to use the evening before to check your speech, equipment and clothes and to get a good night's sleep.

Many people try to allay the night before fears by shutting themselves away and practicing their speech over and over again. Practice once and put the speech out of your mind. If you keep practicing at this late stage you will only increase your nerves.

The eve of the speech is also a good time to check all your visual aids. Make sure that all the equipment is working and that you have all the material that you require.

Take time to lay out your clothes for the occasion, checking all the fine details, such as buttons, shoes cleaned and so on. Take time out to relax, simply resting and focussing your mind for the next day. Make sure that you leave adequate time to set out and before you leave, check that you have everything that you need:

- Your speech-cue cards or crib sheet or script.

- Your spectacles if appropriate.

- A notebook containing the contact number should you get lost or delayed, and also details of the travel arrangements.

- A pen or pencil.

- Some tissues.

- Small change for telephone calls or parking charges.

On arrival

As soon as you arrive, announce yourself to the organizers, get a few minutes of their time and check the following points:

- Have there been any last minute changes of running order-what time are you expected to speak?

- Are the people to whom you will be referring still expected to attend? Check again the names of the people you must mention when proposing a toast.

- Are members of the press or other media expected to attend?

If you are expecting to be introduced, ask to speak to the person who will be performing that function.

Check that he or she has got the facts right, and that they are using only relevant information, you do not want to put the audience to sleep before you have even stood up.

Checking out the venue

At the earliest possible opportunity, pay a visit to room in which you will be speaking. Ensure that the layout is adequate and that all the equipment needed is there. Contact the organizers if there are any discrepancies. Check that the air condition is suitable. If the room feels too hot or cold, make sure that the air conditioning, if any, is adjusted. Listen for audible distractions, such as a bar or kitchen, so that you can prepare for them when you make your speech.

Lighting

Check on the lighting. Make sure that there is ample lighting and that it does not shine in your eyes.

Microphones

For rooms and smaller venues the natural voice can be used. However, for larger halls a microphone is essential. When you are using a microphone keep your head about four inches away when you speak. Avoid any feedback or handling noise.

Appearance

As we mentioned earlier aim at being comfortable and smart. For the woman:

Keep the hair away from the face, so that it is not masked, but retain a soft style. Earrings can soften the face and add interest, but avoid the large dangling variety; they will be a distraction; a colorful scarf or brooch adds a touch of sophistication and interest to the neckline; avoid wearing dull colors unless they are offset by something bright and cheerful; check that your hemlines are straight especially if wearing a full skirt.

For the man

Wear a well fitting suit and shirt with the cuffs just showing below the jacket. The tie should be neatly tied; black shoes are preferable to brown; brown tends to distract the eye. Colored dark socks should be worn, rather than white. Make sure that the socks cover the calves adequately; you should smile as often as possible because this gives the impression of being confident.

Being sociable

When you are satisfied that all the on-the-spot arrangements are complete, you may have time to socialize. You may be asked to join your hosts or gathering members of the audience for a drink. This is a very useful time.

If members of the audience see that you are mingling with them in an affable sort of way, you will reinforce the feeling that you are friendly and relaxed and also sympathetic, someone who takes an interest. It will also enable you to judge the mood of the audience and take your mind off your speech.

Moments before your speech

A few minutes before you are due to speak, begin to prepare yourself. Now is the time to make that final trip to the lavatory or to take a final brisk walk to freshen yourself up. If you have to sit through other peoples speeches be alert and interested. You will probably be just as visible as the person speaking and you must do nothing to distract the audiences attention.

You may also wish to edit your speech in the light of something that has been said. Keep an eye on the time. If the other speaker goes on too long then you may need to edit your speech accordingly.

Walking onto the platform (or standing up)

Make a good first impression. This will work wonders for your confidence. If you are walking up to a platform, adopt an easy gait with your arms swinging naturally and your body straight.

When you are being introduced, look at the introducer and keep an open and alert face. Do not mime a reaction to what the introducer is saying. When the introduction is over, take a deep breath, face the audience and begin. Smile and relax.

If you are using the same space as the previous speaker make sure that you clear up after them-wipe the blackboards, get rid of coffee cups etc. There should be nothing to remind the audience of the previous speech.

Show your audience that you are happy to be there, by being warm and relaxed. Animate your body movements. Positive body language is very important. If you are using a lectern, place your notes on it with a quick glance down, and then look at your audience. Smile as you make your opening remarks. This way you appear much more approachable and attractive.

Focus on your audience. When there is a large audience present, it is sometimes difficult to know where to look when making a speech. If there is strong stage lighting, it is unlikely that you will be able to see your audience, in which case individual eye contact is impossible.

If there is a central exit light at the back of the hall, use that as your main focus point. In between times, the eye can travel to the right hand side of the hall and then the left, always homing back to the exit sign. This gives the illusion of looking at the audience.

Achieving smooth and effective presentations

When you address an audience, in a formal setting, you should always state your name and what it is that you are about to present. This should always head your script. However, if you are going to be introduced by someone else or you are very well known to the audience, you can start in a different way. There are certain fundamental tips that you should take into account when planning. Consider first the mood that your audience is likely to be in. Take the appropriate action for each of the following attitudes of the audience:

- Waiting for you to start. There is no need to capture your audience's attention start when you are ready.

- Expected to disagree with your statements. Do not make matters worse by starting with an announcement that can only worsen the situation.

- Indifferent audience. For this type of audience, you need to be controversial. Start with something that provokes their interest and forces them to listen to you.

After assessing the audience, depending on who is going to be present, you have to decide on the type of opening to use. There are several types of introduction for the situations described above, and here are some effective openings:

- Begin by involving the audience through questions that will make them think about the subject that you are presenting. For example, "Good Morning, were you in a traffic jam this morning and had no way of communicating the fact that you were going to be late? This could be the opener for a talk about some form of communication, for example, the mobile phone.

- Start with an unexpected or controversial statement to seize the attention of the audience.

- Thank the person who introduced you, if he or she is known to the audience. Also, thank the organizers of the event or the people who invited you to give a presentation.

Use these examples as a brief guide and choose the right words for the right situation. It is important to memorize the opening lines because this is the most difficult bit of a presentation. If you get them right then all will usually be plain sailing. If you get them wrong then it may take you time to recover your composure.

Explaining the main points of your presentation

After you have managed to gain their attention you should begin to plan the conveyance of the main part of your text, or script or message. After the introduction, you should tell the audience what you are going to be telling them in the next few minutes.

The following steps should be taken:

- Start by saying a few words about the content of the presentation. Mention the most important points and don't cram the slides with headings of the various sections of the script. Avoid using too many words, especially on the first slide.

- Later in your presentation, give them a reminder of what has been said.

- Bear in mind that people can only concentrate for ten to fifteen minutes. Keep them interested by timing your funny remarks to coincide with the audience's weak moments. Don't spoil your joke by letting them know that you are going to tell one.

- Make sure that your jokes are highly relevant, and don't bring in any old story just for the sake of being funny, as people will wonder about its relevance.

- Another way of getting peoples attention back is to ask them direct questions. If you notice that someone is on the verge of sleeping, you can look at them as you ask the question.

Choosing your closing words

Your last words in the presentation have to be remembered by the audience. Your conclusion is your chance to achieve this. It certainly is not the place to introduce new ideas.

Your conclusion may cover things related to the introduction and the content of the presentation such as what course of action was taken or what can be done in the future. Think hard about what thoughts you want the audience to leave the room with.

Dealing with hecklers

Some people, for whatever reason, come to meetings with the aim of disrupting them. Others may become loud with drink. It is your responsibility to stay in control of the proceedings.

If you have the opportunity before you speak, observe the audience, and note any person likely to disrupt the proceedings. Work hard to grab their attention in particular, once you have started to speak.

The first time that you are heckled, it is best to ignore it, or to smile in response to audience laughter. Try to regain the audience attention immediately. Repeat the last thing that you said to pick up the threads of your speech.

If you are interrupted a second time, be prepared with a put down-witty as opposed to aggressive. Keep your sense of humor at all times and do not lose your cool. This is the aim of the heckler. Try to keep the audience on your side, exposing the heckler as less than savory, and you will succeed in coping.

Only if the heckler becomes abusive should you contemplate having him or her ejected. This should be done quickly and firmly in order to ensure that the proceedings are not terminally disrupted.

Questions from the audience

This is your chance to get positive feedback from the audience. If the occasion is being chaired, and the chairperson is efficient, he or she will monitor the action. Alternatively, engage someone in the audience to set the ball rolling. If a question is being asked too quietly, repeat it for the benefit of the audience. Also, you should rephrase a question that has been poorly expressed. If there is an awkward customer in the audience, try to keep cool. You should think very carefully about how you are going to handle the situation. If it is appropriate you should try asking a few questions.

Accepting compliments

Sometimes, a public speaker gives such a good impression that the audience will applaud or give compliments. It is very important for the speaker to graciously accept these and not to reject them or appear negative. The end of the affair can be so much nicer if all feel appreciated. Remember, be relaxed, be prepared, be spontaneous. Warm to the audience and get them to warm to you and be confident when you are presenting. This will make the whole experience worthwhile and rewarding for all. Use all of the tips that you have picked up throughout the book. Use visual aids to the best effect. Project your voice and involve people.

The end

It's all over! This is time to take stock and consider the whole process, learning from your mistakes and congratulating yourself on your success.

Don't forget, you have done what you set out to do-that is deliver a speech in public. The author hopes that the advice and information contained within this book has helped that process.

Now read the key points from chapter 10 overleaf.

KEY POINTS FROM CHAPTER 10

- All the initial preparations have been for the actual presentation

- Check lighting, microphones and give thought to how you present

- Avoid irritating mannerisms

- Have regard for your appearance

- Your entrance is all important-make a good first impression

- Remember all that you have read and take control

- Gain feedback from your audience!

11

TIME FOR REFLECTION

It is now time to reflect, very briefly, on what has been emphasized throughout this book.

As was stated right at the outset, public speaking is very much an art and a skill that can be mastered by anyone. Some people may be initially better equipped than others for the role of public speaker, but anyone can become an effective speaker and master the art of presentation.

There are two vital ingredients in public speaking and, throughout this book, both aspects have been concentrated upon. *The person* needs to be aware and confident and the *material* needs to be well researched and appropriate to the occasion.

The person needs to be free of nerves and suitably relaxed, aware of his or her body language and also of style, which includes mode of dress.

The material which you are presenting needs to be well researched and organized and appropriate visual aids need to be available to enhance your material. If necessary, use notes and handouts to reinforce what you are saying.

You need to be aware of your voice and of how you deliver the material. Voice development in relation to public speaking is of the utmost importance. The tone, pitch, volume and clarity of your voice all need to be developed, along with the clarity.

Be aware of the setting in which the presentation is to be made, the size and layout plus the general acoustics. Lighting and amplification is also important.

Ensure that you are dressed well, make a good first impression when entering the room and handle the audience confidently and professionally.

The end product of all of the above advice is the delivery of a successful and effective presentation to your audience, whatever that presentation may be. This can be enormously gratifying. However, as we have seen, in order to master the art of public speaking, there is a lot of preparation.

Good luck.

PUBLIC SPEAKING ROLES

Contents

1. Acting as Master of Ceremonies
2. After Dinner Speaking
3. Business Meetings-Informal and Formal
4. Chairing a Meeting
5. Conferences and Conventions
6. Funerals and Memorials
7. Weddings

A master of ceremonies (MC) is employed by the organizers of an event to ensure that its various stages are given some cohesion and that the event itself goes off smoothly and successfully. An MC is usually needed at formal social functions, such as a company dinner, conference or courses.

An MC's duties

The MC does not organize an event and neither does he or she take the place of the chair or figurehead. The essence of the MC's job is that of liaison between all participants.

Behind the scenes the MC is (or should be) totally calm, dealing with any crisis that might arise or any last minute changes, a missing speaker, electrical problems, staff problems and so on. The MC must ensure that everyone knows what is happening when the unforeseen occurs. Guest speakers will be looking to the MC to ensure that speaking conditions are as good as they can be, and to make them feel at home. The MC should meet and greet all Speakers and ensure that their specific needs are attended to.

The public role of the MC is to act as a link between the various stages of the event. At a formal dinner, the MC will shepherd the guests into the dining area, and announce grace and the toasts. At a conference, the MC will ensure that everybody is in the right place at the right time, and introduces the speakers. A good MC will make connections between one speaker and the next, in much the same way as a good speaker connects each part of a speech with a linking paragraph.

The MC will ensure that the audience is not only receptive to what follows, but is also in the right mood. A lively audience may need to be quelled in order that they might be better able to take in some serious facts and figures. A subdued audience may need to be jollied up in preparation for some light-hearted entertainment. An audience whose members are likely to fall asleep after dinner will need to be woken up!

The content of an MC's speech is information. The MC must be concise and to the point, and must be sure that all of the facts that they have are right. The MC must not allow their personality to upstage other speakers.

In moments of crisis, the MC must be prepared to ad-lib, disguising any tension in the situation, and keeping the audience occupied until the event can get under way again. The skill of impromptu speaking is therefore a necessary one to acquire if you are to fill this role.

The role of Master of Ceremonies is unenviable. Very few people notice when things run smoothly, everyone notices when things go wrong. The MC is a focal point for emotions when things do go wrong. The good MC will allow their own personalities to 'disappear' in the process of liaison and introduction. You will need to be a strong mature character to take on and maintain the role of MC. It is, however, an invaluable role for developing the role of public speaking.

The majority of formal dinner occasions are hosted by organizations such as companies, clubs, associations or charities. As with many other social occasions, almost all after dinner speeches take the form of toasts and replies. In some instance, a guest speaker will also be invited, and in this case, an introduction will usually be given.

Organizing after-dinner speakers

It will normally be the role of the chairman to see that the list of toasts and speakers is drawn up, and that each speaker is introduced in the correct order. It may be undesirable for the chairman to be the person to introduce each speaker. An alternative is to employ a Master of Ceremonies to perform these functions. Whoever is in control of the proceedings, it is vital that they have a good sense of timing and also brevity. The speaker must know how to speed the proceedings if they are flagging and how to wait for the right moment before moving on.

The MC or toast-maker will ask the company to stand up while grace is said. After grace the guests sit down and the meal can begin. Whether or not you say grace, of course, depends on the nature of the guests. It may not always be appropriate.

Toasting the host

At normal functions, the host is normally an organization. It usually falls to one of the guests to propose a toast to the host. It is necessary to know something about the host, and to keep in mind the reason for the dinner. If you are not a member of the host organization, you might be able to get a copy of their annual report or some other publication which will give you some idea of what they do. You may be from a related organization, in which case you can draw comparisons between the two. Always try to mention the guests of honor if there are any. If not, the chairman or president of the host organization will count as the most important person, and you should mention him or her. Again, it is diplomatic, not to say wise, to know something about the person who will be responding to the toast, and to mention him or her in the proposing toast.

Toasting the guests

A member of the host organization is expected to propose a toast to the guests. This involves introducing the guests of honor to the company and welcoming them and all the other guests to the event. Mention guests in order of precedence, include those who have been invited because they hold particular positions or as a recognition of certain services or successes.

Introduce these guests individually and elaborate on their achievements (in their official capacity). Other important guests may include titled people, prominent business people, government officials and so on. Remember to use the correct form of address when mentioning important people.

After singling out individuals, next mention all the other guests. The company may be divided into groups (i.e. business groupings such as departments so take advantage of this and find something good to say about each.

Toasting the chairman

The toast is to the head of the host organization-its chairman or president. It requires the most preparation, because it is the most individual toast. The person who is proposing the toast should most definitely know something about his career and character. Mention the personal qualities that have been of benefit to the organization, and the successful changes or projects that he or she has initiated whilst with the organization. Try to achieve balance between admiration and humor and try to avoid being over familiar or sycophantic. Avoid any subject that could be a potential embarrassment.

Civic Toasts

This toast is proposed when the civic head of a town or city is attending, such as the Mayor. It need only be a short toast to which the civic head will respond.

The most important thing to remember is that the civic head is attending as a representative of a community and not as an individual so keep any toast politically neutral.

Toast to the ladies

This toast stands as a monument to the days when women attended formal dinners as escorts to their husbands. These days, it is likely that such escorts are both male and female. If this toast is included, it is more appropriate to use it as an opportunity to thank the partners of company or club members, perhaps for their support over the last year.

Replies

Each of the above toasts require replies which should be made immediately following the relevant toast. The purpose is to thank the proposer and make a short speech.

Reply on behalf of the host

This is normally made by a member of the host organization. Find out something about the person who proposed the toast. Introduce him or her, offer your thanks for their kind words, and perhaps elaborate on what they have said. You may like to tell the assembled company why this person was chosen to propose the toast. You may also like to tell the audience why you have been asked to respond. Wind up the reply by repeating your thanks on behalf of the host organization.

Reply on behalf of the guests

Once again, thank the proposer of the toast to the guests, and find something comfortable to say to him or her. The main task is to show that the guests are enjoying their evening, so be humorous if you can.

Chairman's reply

On many occasions, this is the most important speech of the evening. The chairman should use it to mention the successes of the past year and to perhaps to give some idea of where the organization is going in the coming year. Avoid giving lists and make sure that you single out some members of the organization by name. It is also the chairman's job to thank the organizers of the dinner.

Introducing a guest speaker

Some organizations engage the services of a guest speaker-someone who may be connected with the organization, or who may have something of special interest to say. In most cases, a guest speaker will be a professional engaged to amuse and to keep the audience happy.

If you are asked to introduce the guest speaker, make sure that you find out who he or she is and why they have been invited. A person will always need an introduction. Even if the speaker is the President of the USA you must make an effort to connect the speaker with the event and give audience a reason to listen. Most of all, the introducers job is to welcome the speaker and set them off on the right foot.

The guest speaker

The primary objective of an after-dinner speaker's appearance is to be amusing and the major imperative is to be relevant to the occasion and topical. The brief is normally very wide-ranging and so you will need to put in some work to define the subject for your speech. You might take it from the activities of the host organization, and include scandals and goings-on in the organizations industry or sector. You might want to mention recent stories in the media. Find out as much as you can about the interests of the audience so that you can connect with their interests and concerns.

It is also useful to know something about the chairman, so that you can include a short anecdote.

The conditions under which many after dinner speeches are given are quite often difficult. The audience may by this time be fairly well oiled and so you may encounter hecklers or other disturbances. You may also find that the audience is scattered about the room, seated at tables in groups. This means that you will have to work hard to draw audiences attention away from the events taking place in each group and to focus their attention on you. It often happens that each table may form its own little society with its own humorists and leaders. Try to pick them out early on and control their behaviour with eye contact and perhaps the occasional mention.

Vote of thanks

It is customary for a member of the host organization to thank a guest speaker on behalf of the organization. It is not necessary to summarize the whole of the foregoing speech simply to show that you, as a representative of the audience found it interesting and amusing. This is one situation in which you will need to make some notes and be ready to improvise.

If the speech has been a great success, say so, but avoid being over lavish with your praise. Even if the speech has been a total flop, do try hard to be sincere in your thanks. The vote of thanks usually ends with a call for applause.

Business meetings-formal and informal

The vast majority of meetings take place within the context of business. They are part of the internal and external communications process that is so important to any company. Business meetings are either formal or informal. The only real difference between the two is one of context-the skills required are the same. To perform well, you need to be capable of persuading and able to speak coherently at a moment's notice.

Preparation for business meetings

Most formal business meetings are heralded well in advance. You should be told the purpose of the meeting and who is going to be present, and why. If you do not have an agenda, you need to ask the following questions:

- When and where is the meeting to be held?
- What is the purpose of the meeting?
- Who will be present and what is their status?
- Have the other participants been briefed with the necessary information?
- Why are you being asked to attend?
- How long is the meeting expected to go on for?

A meeting could have a number of purposes: problem solving, decision making, selling (ideas as well as products) or transmitting information. Work out which you will be expected to do and plan your contribution accordingly.

Knowing who the other participants are will enable you to build up a picture of their needs and interests, which you will have to take into account. This is most likely to be a mixed group, at least in terms of the corporate hierarchy. Understanding what these different concerns are will enable you to speak more effectively and, if necessary, be more persuasive.

Do not aim your speech at one group only. It may be tempting to level your arguments at your superiors, on the assumption that they are the people with the power to improve your career prospects. However, this will not only irritate your peer colleagues and subordinates, it is also likely to be detrimental to your cause.

In order to have proposals of any sort accepted, you will need to have them agreed by all the people they affect. Therefore, consider all members of your audience as equals.

It is important that you know how much the other participants know about the business in hand. If they know very little, you may have to spend time presenting information before you can move on to a discussion of the issues. If they have been fully briefed you will waste time going over old ground. If it seems that there is information that participants should have in advance, suggest to the meeting organizer that it is circulated.

When you know who the other participants are, and you have found out their concerns and the information they already have, you should be able to start making assumptions about their attitude towards the subject in hand:

- Will there be a consensus of opinion on the subject?
- Who will be against and why?
- Who can you count on as allies to agree with you and support you?

Finding out why you have been asked to attend is vital. You may be expected to speak on behalf of your department, or to advise because you have specific expertise. You may be expected to report on the progress of your project, or to explain problems or make recommendations. Remember to formulate a statement of your own objectives with the other participants in mind, and when you have finished preparing your contribution, check that you have addressed as many of the concerns of others as you can.

The art of persuading

It could be that the objective of your speech is to persuade-to sell an idea or other products to participants. Here are a few tips on persuasion:

- Understand the other parties stand point: gain their sympathy by showing that you understand
- Establish a need: you cannot reach a solution if the other party does not agree that there is a problem
- Give suggestions and explain their advantages: relate your solution/idea to the needs of the other party, interpret exactly how it will change their life/working conditions/effectiveness
- Gloss over areas of minor disagreement: do not let them get in the way of the major issue; broad agreement is better than no agreement
- Emphasize areas of agreement
- Encourage a conclusion; define it and allow the other party to agree without losing face.
- Avoid coercion and the hard sell
- Show that you are committed and enthusiastic about your idea/product/solution.

Discussion in meetings

Discussion is common to almost all meetings. Participants will air their views and thrash out solutions to problems. Discussion is vital to the communications process but unfocussed discussion is a waste of time and money.

A discussion is like a speech, except that it is made not by one speaker but by several. Efficient discussion relies on the participants being well informed and able to put their points coherently and concisely. You performance in discussion is just as important as your ability to make a prepared presentation. Points to remember for discussion:

- Be prepared: read the agenda and other information. Make notes on points you would like to raise.

- Listen attentively to the other speakers. Try to identify their viewpoint. If you can, test you assumption by asking questions. Make notes.

- Your body language should convey that you are alert and open to new ideas.

- Never whisper while another person is speaking and don't interrupt.

- Show that you value other people's ideas and that you value their point of view.

- If a person has already made the point that you wanted to make, say that you agree with him or her and perhaps add your own view.

- If you are introducing a new line of reasoning or a new idea, make sure that you relate it to the subject under discussion, in the same way that you would link two stages in a speech.

In general, it is the chair's role to direct the discussion and to make regular summaries to keep the meeting moving forward. If this does not happen, it might fall to you to do this.

Meetings cost time and money and each participant is being paid to attend and they are all putting aside their work to do so. Each person has to do his or her bit to ensure that the meeting runs efficiently. A good public speaker is invaluable within this context.

Chairing a meeting

This particular form of public speaking requires special qualities in the person who chooses to accept it. Most important of all is the ability to listen when you really want to speak.

Whatever the type of the meeting, whether formal in a context where the services of a chairman are required by law, or informal, such as departmental meetings, it is essential that the chairman remains impartial and devotes his or her energy to guiding the meeting, controlling speakers and ensuring an outcome. The chairman should never comment on the substances of speeches being put to the meeting, either for or against.

Make sure that both sides get a good hearing. You will soon be able to pick out the strong personalities among those attending, and to control them, whilst at the same time giving those who are not confident their say. You may wish to invoke the rule that a person cannot speak on any given subject or motion. If you find this useful, state this rule at the beginning of the meeting.

The only time it is legitimate for the chair to show which side he or she is on is when a casting vote is needed. If you cannot be impartial-perhaps you have a special interest in the matter in hand-you should consider delegating the chair to someone else or not accept it in the first place.

Conducting business

The aim of all meetings is to get through as much business as possible. You must be able to chair effectively and continually bring people back to the point. One way of doing this is to set a time limit on each speech at the start of the meeting and be firm when that limit has been reached. Always aim to move on quickly whilst at the same time aiming not to cut people off mid-stream. This requires a certain skill and it is one that is gained by practice.

Formal meetings

Formal meetings-AGM's for example-are governed by law and the rules of the company or corporation. It is essential that the person chairing a meeting understands these laws and rules and regulations.

The first responsibility of the chairman is to ensure that the proper notice of a meeting is given, according to the body's regulations. There must be enough people in attendance to be able to conduct business. The chairman will welcome those attending and state the purpose of the meeting. He or she may also read through an agenda. The chair will then call on the secretary to read the minutes of the previous meeting and when this is complete ask whether the minutes represent an accurate record of the previous meeting and whether there are matters arising.

Finally, the business of the meeting can get under way. When the meeting is finished, the chairman will announce the date and time of the next meeting and declare the meeting closed.

Informal meetings

The vast majority of meetings are informal. They may be meetings between a client and a supplier firm, or between members of different departments. Informal meetings are not bound by the same rigid rules that guide formal meetings, but the char still needs to be in command, and still needs the same respect in order to see fair play and to se that things are done.

As with formal meetings, it is the chairman's business to ensure that the right people attend, and that all the relevant information is circulated beforehand if necessary. During the meeting, the chairman should guide the discussion and summarize when necessary and bring matters to a conclusion. After the meeting, he or she should also circulate notes of the meeting, with details of the action agreed upon.

Although the meeting is informal, the chair still has to command respect and guide the meeting to its logical conclusion without undue personal involvement.

The role of a Chairman is a very important role indeed, requires certain skills and to be able to chair effectively is the mark of an effective public speaker.

Speaking to a conference or convention is similar to lecturing. The main difference is that the audience is likely to be made up of knowledgeable people. This will mean that your speech will have to be crafted so that it is interesting and not stultifying.

The kind of speech that you make at a conference will obviously depend on the type of conference and the purpose of the gathering. Obviously, if you are going to give a speech at a conference then you will need to find out all the detail that you can.

You may be there to sell your product or idea to people in your industry. You must, in this case, bring to bear all your persuasive skills. Alternatively, you may have been invited to pass on information, so you should aim to do just that. Use visual aids if you think that they will help increase understanding.

Keeping the audience interested

If you are speaking on the first day of a conference, there will usually be a capacity audience full of intent listeners. However, there is also the fact that you may be booked to speak at less advantageous times, after lunch, when people feel sleepy or early in the morning when some might have hangovers and so on. At these times, the audience will be less than attentive. Check the time when you are supposed to speak and work harder to enthuse your audience if you are booked to speak at one of these times.

Using your time

When you are not speaking, use your time to listen to other speakers. This is not only polite but will also benefit you in that you can pick up crucial tips. You can also gauge your audience and tailor your own speech beforehand. When no speeches are scheduled, socialize with other delegates. This way, you can continue doing your homework.

Conventions and conferences-Compiling a checklist

Research and prepare your conference speech as you would any other full-length presentation. Some important points to remember are:

- Have you written and delivered material for the chairperson to use when introducing you?

- Have you double-checked the details of when and where you are expected to make your appearance?

- Have you checked that you have your notes and visual aids with you?

- Have you checked personal arrangements such as hotel accommodation, travel, fees and expenses?

- Have you checked the conditions at the venue?

On the day:

- Check that your visual aids are in position and that all necessary equipment is working

- Check the venue. Make sure that the air conditioning is working to your advantage.

- Ask a steward to shepherd the audience into a compact group at the front and centre of the room, so that it is easier to make contact with them and mould their group responses.

- Clear the room of odds and ends left by other speakers-paper cups, used flip charts, anything that will distract attention.

For both speakers and audience alike, conferences and conventions can be enjoyable events. They are invaluable for communicating to other members of the profession. You should capitalize on this opportunity to raise awareness of your work, product or thinking and to learn from other speakers.

Probably the most difficult speaking occasion you will encounter is that of the funeral. This is because you will have cope with your own grief and also that of others. You will also be voicing the deepest emotions of those around you.

Funerals and memorials may be slightly different. A funeral service is normally more personal and immediate than a memorial, because the grief is still fresh in peoples minds and the people attending are likely to be relatives and close friends. A memorial may take place on the anniversary of a persons death and may include people who perhaps were not so close.

Funerals

At a funeral, the most important people are the immediate family. Find out what they would like you to say and comply with their requests. Keep your speech short and simple, personal and sincere and convey the essence of the character of the deceased. Do not over-dramatize or declaim.

The structure of a funeral speech

- Introduce the occasion. Direct the formal address to the close family, using their Christian names if appropriate.

- Describe the deceased, mentioning some good times or endearing qualities: perhaps he or she was a pillar of the community and it might be appropriate to mention status and achievements.

- Address sympathy to the family and pledge your support.
- Sum up with a few choice words, for example, the deceased was much loved, is greatly missed and so on.

Never speak ill of the dead-even if you cannot find a decent thing to say about a person and you have a personal grievance. If it is a problem, you should refuse to speak.

Do not allow yourself to be so overcome with emotion that you break down. Never drink before your speech.

In Memoriam

A memorial is likely to be less overwhelming than a funeral. It is more of a celebration of a dead person s life and work, but it is still a solemn occasion. The structure above may be adapted to a memorial by adding more anecdotes, which may be even more humorous. Try to strike a balance between portraying the private and public person, and remember to elaborate your relationship with the deceased.

Weddings

For many people, weddings are the only time in their lives where they will be asked to give a speech. Wedding speeches are most often given by novices who suffer from nerves and self-doubt. However, this is one of the most important days in the life of newly weds and it is crucial that you make a good speech.

The form

It is usual to have three speeches, and all are toasts. The first toast is proposed by the brides father, or a close family friend or relative. He or she proposes the health of the bride and groom. Next, the groom replies, and proposes a toast to the bridesmaids. Finally, the best man replies on behalf of the bridesmaids.

As with all things, time has changed the usual customs and women are now beginning to assert themselves and make a speech after the groom has finished. Also, best men are also joined by best women. Each of these speeches need to be prepared in advance and delivered as one would deliver any speech. The following are suggestions for each speech.

The bride and groom

The toast to the bride and groom should express happiness at the occasion and wish them both luck in their new life. It is customary to compliment the bride on her appearance and to compliment the groom on his luck.

You may wish to add an anecdote from having known the bride so long, or you may have a funny story about the first time you met the groom. Finish by asking the guests to raise their glasses and drink to the health of the bride and groom.

The things not to do at a wedding speech

- Never make jokes about the bride or mother in law. This is pathetic and outdated

- Never make remarks which are in bad taste

- Avoid smut, innuendo or references to past partners

- Don't use the opportunity to score points

- Keep in mind that this is the bride and grooms special day, so only add to their pleasure.

The Bridesmaids

Next up is the groom, who thanks the proposer of the previous toast and in turn proposes the toast to the bridesmaids. The groom usually compliments the bride on her appearance and thanks her for consenting to marry him. He usually compliments on his good fortune on having found her. He thanks his best man for supporting him, and for working so hard to ensure that the day has run so smoothly. Sometimes, the groom also thanks the bride's family for allowing him the honour of marrying her.

However, this is increasingly seen as sexist and outdated. The groom, however, should at least thank the bride's family for accepting him in their home.

The groom then proceeds to tell a few anecdotes before he turns to the subject of the bridesmaids. He should compliment them on how well turned out they are and thank them for attending his wife so well. He will finish by proposing a toast to the bridesmaids.

The main event

The best mans speech is usually the highlight of the wedding. The audience is expected to laugh and the speech is usually timed at between five to ten minutes. Start by thanking the groom on behalf of the bridesmaids. Add your compliments to both them and the bride.

The usual course of events after this is to say something about your relationship with the groom, and to recount some lively stories about your youth together. If you did not know each other when you were younger then tell a few stories about recent events. While it is expected that you will embarrass the groom slightly, it is important that you do not overstep the mark and ruin his reputation.

Best man's humour

You should not allow your speech to turn into a string of jokes, just for the sake of getting laughs. Never make jokes in bad taste and keep in mind the age and profile of those present. Avoid lewd comments. At the end of your speech, read any telegrams or other communications of good wishes, and introduce any special guests. Keep this section short, as the audience might become restless.

Other speeches

If the bride and groom take a decision to vary this format, they should tell everyone involved and work out who is going to propose which toast. If the bride wishes to make a speech, she usually takes the opportunity to propose the toast to the people who have make the wedding such a special occasion.

While you are quite at liberty to arrange for as many speeches as you wish, avoid allowing them to go on for too long. It is highly likely that alcohol, food, endless speeches and so on, will all have taken their toll.